Preface

This volume compiles the first three books of *One Story A Day For Early Readers*, a series of twelve books designed to develop a love of reading in children ages 8-10, now divided into four volumes.

Written by a team of professional writers, these books comprise high-interest topics and motivational content that make children excited about reading.

The stories are based on everyday life, funny tales of friendship and family, fables from around the world, and stories about nature, science, and history.

One Story A Day fosters children's total development through the joy of reading. Both the content and structure of the books encourage children to read every day. Controlled vocabulary and targeted illustrations make the stories easy to understand.

There is supplemental audio online for each book, with all stories narrated in clear, natural voices by professional actors.

This series can be used in a variety of settings and with many different approaches. The stories will bring the joy of words and reading to the ears and minds of children at a crucial stage in their development.

Sit back, relax, and discover the pleasure of reading!

Book 1 for January .... p. 1

Book 2 for February .... p. 65

Book 3 for March .... p. 125

Written by: Leonard Judge, Scott Paterson, Jennifer Burrows, Gail Marshall

Illustrators: Meredith Luce, Meiling Liu, Junpo Cao, Jasmine Vincente, Steve Hutchison

Producer: Meizhen Dang

Editors: Leonard Judge, Nanma Bar-David, Susanne Wilkins

Copyright © 2024 DC Canada Education Publishing

Published by: DC Canada Education Publishing

www.dc-canada.ca

• •

All rights reserved. No part of this book may be reproduced in any form or by any electronic or mechanical means without written permission of the copyright owner.

We acknowledge the financial support of the Government of Canada for our publishing activities.

One Story A Day For Early Readers - Books 1-3
ISBN: 978-1-77205-935-9

One Story A Day
for Early Readers

(Book 1 for January)

DC Canada Education Publishing

Table of Contents

1	Where Does Milk Come from?	2
2	Grandma's Moving Day	4
3	A Little Artist	6
4	Snow or Not	8
5	Do Fish Breathe Water?	10
6	Where Is My Pen?	12
7	When the Earth Shakes	14
8	Just the Way You Are	16
9	My Mother's Chair	18
10	Where Is Danny?	20
11	Earth Day	22
12	Needles Don't Hurt	24
13	Colours	26
14	Open Your Eyes	28
15	The Picture	30
16	Healthy Heart	32

17	Baby Jessie	34
18	The Little Red Teapot	36
19	The Party	38
20	The Three Sisters	40
21	Baseball or Piano?	42
22	The Missing Gloves	44
23	The Gentle Giant	46
24	Protect Mom's Belly	48
25	How Old Are You?	50
26	Molly Can't Fall Asleep	52
27	Working with Dad	54
28	What to Be	56
29	Big Green Ball	58
30	Kenny's Adventure	60
31	Baby Brother	62

Where Does Milk Come from?

Billy is six years old. He visits his uncle and aunt every summer. They live on a farm.

They have cows, chickens, sheep, and a big horse on the farm. Billy loves all the animals.

This summer, he is going to learn how to milk a cow. Wow! His friends cannot believe it.

"We get our milk from the store," they say. "But our friend is going to get it from a cow."

Billy laughs. "Milk does not come from the store," he says. "Milk comes from a cow."

His friends do not believe him. But his teacher says, "Yes, milk comes from cows. Cows eat grass. They change the grass into milk. The farmer sells the milk. And we buy it in the stores."

The teacher tells them one more thing. "Did you know that cows have four stomachs?" The kids are surprised. But it's true!

Grandma's Moving Day

The day had come. Grandma was moving out of her big house. I was sad. I had a lot of memories in that house.

I asked where Grandma was moving to. My dad just said, "Somewhere nearby. Don't worry."

But I was worried. I spent a lot of time with Grandma. I did not want to see her any less. In fact, I wanted to see her more.

I could tell that no one wanted to tell me because they knew I would be sad. "It must be far away," I thought to myself.

We got all of Grandma's things in the truck. I sat beside her in the car. We talked the whole time.

After a while, the truck stopped. I looked out to see her new home.

It was our house! Grandma was coming to live with us.

3
A Little Artist

Irene is only three years old. But to her parents, she is already a little artist.

At their home, her paintings cover the walls of all the rooms—even the bathroom.

"A child's creativity is beyond your imagination," her mom always says. "And she can be highly productive too."

One time, her mother counted all of Irene's drawings. Irene had used nearly 500 sheets of paper in just one month!

Most of her drawings are of animals: birds, rabbits, turtles, and even raccoons. All the animals in her paintings are in groups of three—a father, a mother, and a baby.

That's how it is in little Irene's world.

4 Snow or Not

When I was young, my family always seemed short of food. We were poor. My brothers and sisters and I were hungry all of the time.

We didn't have much flour. And sugar was rare. You know, with flour and sugar, our mom could make delicious treats. Flour and sugar were signs of wealth to us.

When it snowed in winter, I always wondered, "Why doesn't it snow flour?"

"Or sugar," my young brother would correct me.

We imagined how happy we would be if it snowed flour and sugar—precious white flour and sugar!

When we grew up, we laughed about how silly we were. If it snowed flour and sugar, there would be big problems in the world. We would not be able to survive very long!

Do Fish Breathe Water?

Joey has a pet. Her name is Goldie. She lives in a bowl. Goldie is a fish—a shiny goldfish.

Once a week, Joey takes Goldie out of her bowl. He cleans her bowl so she can grow strong and healthy.

When Joey's parents gave him Goldie, they said, "You will have to learn to take care of her." So, Joey started learning a lot about fish.

Joey used to think fish did not breathe. "How can they breathe in the water?" he thought. "When I swim, I cannot breathe if I put my head under the water!"

But fish get air in a different way. They have "gills" on the sides of their heads.

Joey learned that water has oxygen in it. The water passes through the gills. The fish get their oxygen from the water.

When Joey cleans the fish bowl, he puts Goldie in a small glass of water. That way, she can breathe while he cleans her home.

Where Is My Pen?

Amy is not happy. She cannot find her favourite pen!

She looks all over the house. She looks under the bed. She looks in her desk. She looks in the kitchen and in her book bag. But she cannot find it.

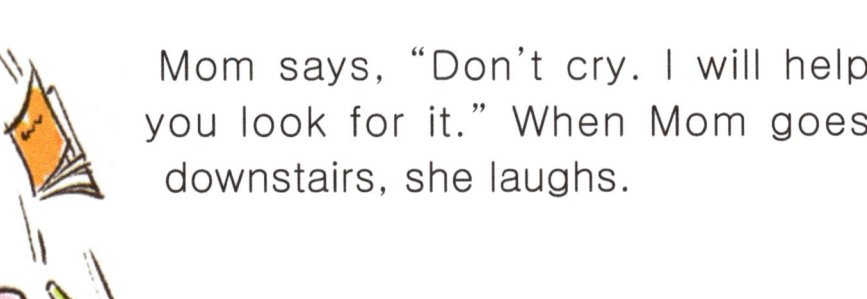

Amy is really upset. Amy wants to cry. She cries to her mother, "Mom, my pen is lost!"

Mom says, "Don't cry. I will help you look for it." When Mom goes downstairs, she laughs.

"Why are you laughing, Mom?"

Mom says, "Check behind your ear." And as Amy checks her ear, she finds her pen. She had put it there earlier.

Now she is happy.

When the Earth Shakes

It was a day Tony would never forget. He was playing with his friends in the yard. All of a sudden, there was a strange noise. Then, everything started to shake.

Tony saw that his house was moving. Dogs were barking. Chickens were running around in fear. A horse was standing upright on its back legs. What was it? Tony had no idea.

Some of the kids fell down and others were trying to keep from falling.

A woman ran outside and shouted, "Hurry! It's an earthquake. Get away from the building!"

Tony was so scared that he couldn't move. The woman grabbed him and led him away from the building.

It was his first earthquake.

Tony was shocked to learn that the ground he stood on every day could shake! And that shaking could hurt a lot of people.

Just the Way You Are

Sometimes, it is fun being tall. Sometimes, it is not.

Sure, I can always reach things for my mom, dad, sister or teacher. But sometimes, I would rather be short.

I am always the tallest one in pictures! Sometimes, I wish people didn't notice me as much.

Another boy, John, is the shortest kid in our class. He told me that he wished people didn't notice him as much either!

We became friends because we feel the same, in a strange way.

When we play basketball together, people say, "It's a lot of fun to watch a game with the school's tallest and shortest boys on the same team."

It's true, you know. You can't be too tall or too short. It's just the way you are.

My Mother's Chair

My mother has a favourite chair. She got it from her mother. This chair is very old. It is the only one of its kind because my grandfather made it.

One day, my brother pushed me when we were running through the house. I started to slip and ran right into the chair. One of the legs came off!

We were shocked. We could not speak. I called my dad at work. He came home and glued it together. He put a clamp on it to hold it in place while the glue dried.

My mom came home. We hoped she wouldn't notice, but she saw the clamp on the chair.

We told her what had happened. She was very upset.

Luckily, the chair was fixed.

Even though that old chair is much stronger now, we are not allowed to run in the house anymore!

10 Where Is Danny?

Danny is hiding from his friends today. Usually, Danny and his friends, Jenny and Eddy, play on the playground after school. But not today.

When classes ended, Jenny and Eddy came to meet Danny as usual. But he was not there. Where was he?

On Danny's desk, they found a piece of paper with some writing on it.

They picked up the note and read it. "Hello my friends. I'm going to a place where we have lunch every day. Find me there."

Eddy scratched his head. "Where is that?" he asked.

"It's the place where we eat," said

Jenny. "It's the cafeteria!"

They ran to the school cafeteria. And yes, there he was! Danny was sweeping the floor, and a few other boys and girls were washing the tables, chairs, and counters!

Right away, they rolled up their sleeves and joined the cleaning with Danny.

Earth Day

The first Earth Day was on April 22, 1970. It was in the United States.

A man named Mr. Nelson started it. He wanted people to take care of the earth. People worked on cleaning the land, water and air. Some people picked up trash. Other people planted trees and flowers.

The second Earth Day was on April 22, 1990. This time, people all over the world took part. Now we celebrate Earth Day every year on April 22.

People in Australia clean beaches. People in Jordan and Canada plant trees. People in Russia plant gardens. People in Sweden visit farms. On one Earth Day, people in Japan made soap and postcards out of trash.

What will you do on Earth Day this year?

Needles Don't Hurt

Gena is scared. Today, she is going to see the doctor. She is going to get a needle.

Gena does not like needles. "It will hurt," she cries. "I don't want to get a needle."

Mom says, "Getting a needle is good for you. It will help you stay healthy."

The doctor is wearing a white coat. She has a nice smile. The doctor looks at Gena and says, "Don't be afraid. The needle will not hurt. Everyone gets needles."

Gena holds out her arm. She is still scared.

"Close your eyes and think of something funny," says the doctor. Gena closes her eyes, thinking. She feels a small pinch on her arm.

"There now," says the doctor. "You are a good girl."

It is over. Gena laughs. She is not scared of needles anymore.

13 Colours

Jake got out a piece of paper. Then he found a paintbrush and four colours of paint. He had red, yellow, blue, and white.

He painted a red boat floating on blue water. He painted a yellow sun peaking through white clouds.

"I need orange for my picture," said Jake. He mixed some of the red with some of the yellow. It made a nice shade of orange.

"That's better," said Jake. "But I need green too." He mixed some of the yellow with some of the blue. It made a nice shade of green.

"That's better," said Jake. "What about purple? I need purple as well." He mixed some of the blue with some of the red. It made a nice shade of purple.

"Much better," said Jake. "Now I'm ready to paint a rainbow."

 # Open Your Eyes

My grandpa always says, "The world is a beautiful place if you just open your eyes." Now I know what he means.

One time, my friend's family invited me to go with them for a balloon ride.

We all got in the basket. Then we started to lift off the ground. I got scared and closed my eyes.

When I opened one eye, I saw the trees below us. I quickly shut my eyes again.

Suddenly, my friend yelled, "Look!" A huge flock of geese was flying right by us.

For a while, we blew right along with them. It was the most beautiful thing I had ever seen!

It was an amazing sight. Just imagine... all I had to do was open my eyes.

Good advice, Grandpa!

The Picture

My uncle took a picture during his trip to Asia. It was taken on the sidewalk of a busy street.

In the picture is a boy with a pencil and a notebook. He is working on his homework. There is no desk and no chair. He is using a stool as his desk.

Around the boy are his father and mother. The father is

pointing to the book, trying to help. The mother is smiling and watching them closely. Beside them is their family business—a bicycle repair stand.

It seems that the parents do not have much education. But you can see that they care strongly about their son's school work. Their eyes are filled with hope.

Bicycles, cars, buses and people are passing by in the picture. But this family is not disturbed by the noise. To the family, the son's studies seem to be the centre of the world.

I was really touched by this picture.

Healthy Heart

Thump. Thump. That is the sound of your heart beating. What an amazing muscle! It works all day. It works all night.

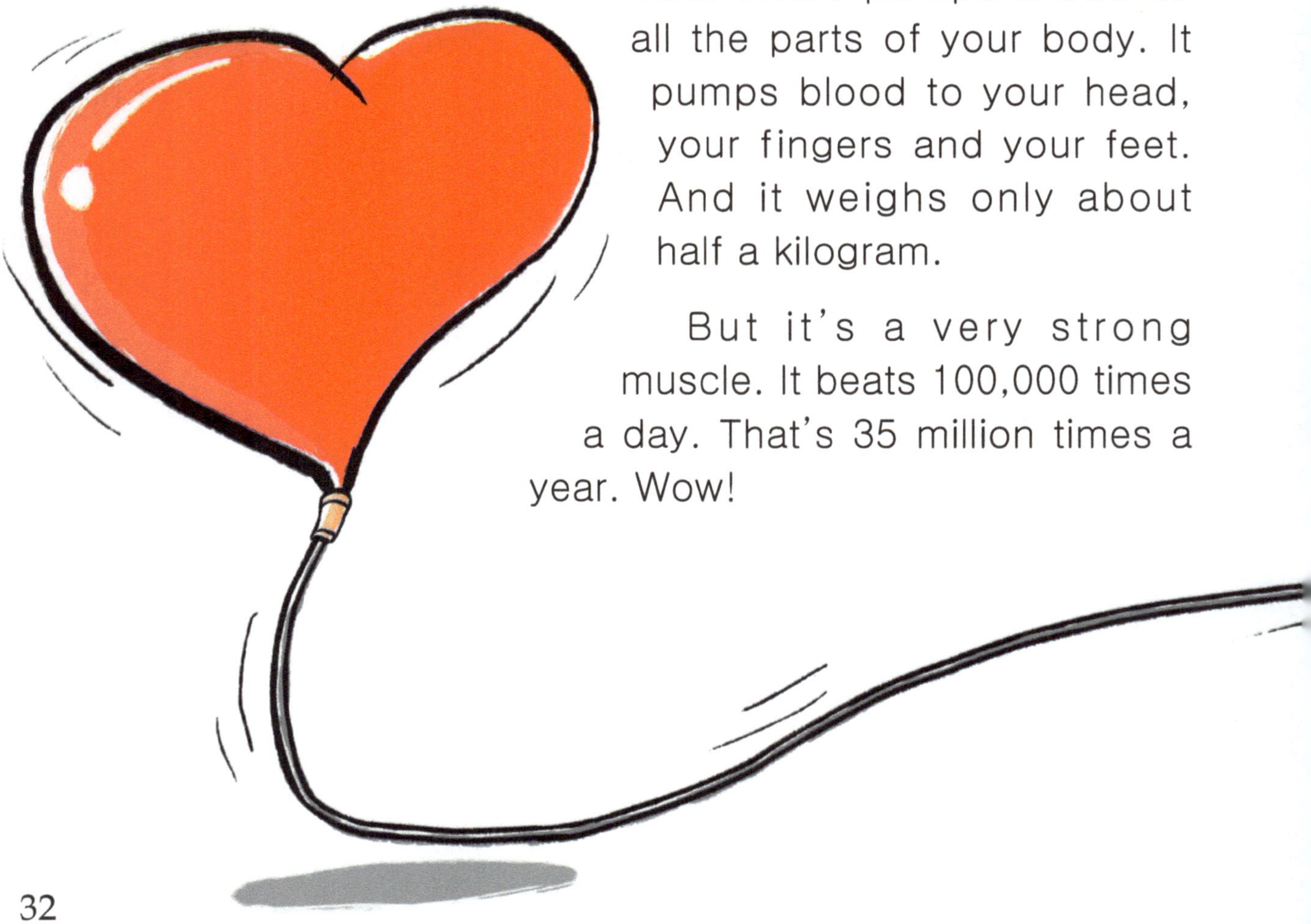

Your heart pumps blood to all the parts of your body. It pumps blood to your head, your fingers and your feet. And it weighs only about half a kilogram.

But it's a very strong muscle. It beats 100,000 times a day. That's 35 million times a year. Wow!

In your lifetime, your heart will beat about two and a half billion times. You know what else is really amazing? Your heart does all of this without you even giving it a thought. It just keeps working.

Most hearts beat about 70 times every minute. See for yourself. Put your hand on your wrist. Feel your heart beating. Now, count how many times it beats in a minute.

Take care of your heart. Eat well. Sleep well. And get lots of exercise. That way, your heart will be strong and keep on beating.

17

Baby Jessie

Everyone was waiting for Jessie and her parents to arrive. "They'll be here soon!"

"Can Jessie and I play games together?" asked Laurie.

"Not yet," answered Mom. "Jessie is still a baby, you know."

"It takes a long time for a baby to turn into a kid, doesn't it?" asked Laurie. Mom laughed, "Yes, it does."

"Then she isn't good for much yet," said Laurie.

Dad laughed, "I don't think her parents would agree with that. They kind of like her."

A moment later, Jessie and her parents finally arrived.

Jessie started crying because she didn't recognize Laurie and her family.

"She really isn't worth much," thought Laurie. But she didn't say this out loud.

Laurie then showed Jessie the box of toys. She shook a rattle at her. Jessie laughed.

"I guess maybe she is worth a little bit," thought Laurie as her eyes lit up.

18

The Little Red Teapot

Last winter, I had a bad cold. I could hardly breathe through my nose. In the morning, my mother brought me a little red teapot.

"Tea? I don't like tea!" I said.

"I know," Mom said. "But tea is one of the best things you can drink. It's very healthy. This is a special tea for when you are sick."

There was no way out. I brought the cup to my lips and took a small sip. The tea was strong and bitter.

I knew my mom was trying to help me. So I took another sip. Within a few hours, I could breathe through my nose again!

Was it the tea? I don't know. But I do know that the next time I'm sick, I'll be looking for that little red teapot again!

19

The Party

One hot summer day, Mouse decided to have a party.

Mouse walked over to Beaver's house. "Beaver, please come to my party. I'll be serving bananas," said Mouse.

"Bananas? I'll only come if you serve oranges," said Beaver.

"Okay," said Mouse. "My friends will like oranges. I'll make sure to pick some up."

Next, Mouse walked to Rabbit's house. "Rabbit, please come to my party. I'll be serving oranges," said Mouse.

"Oranges? I'll only come if you serve apples," said Rabbit.

"Okay," said Mouse. But he was puzzled.

Mouse then walked to Squirrel's house. "Squirrel, please come to my party. I'll be serving apples," said Mouse.

"Apples? I'll only come if you serve bananas," said Squirrel.

"Alright!" exclaimed Mouse.

Mouse knew exactly what to do. He cut up bananas, oranges and apples. Then, he mixed them all in a bowl. "Now all of my guests will be happy!"

20

The Three Sisters

(based on a Canadian Native story)

Eddy and Casey did not like eating vegetables. They liked meat and fish. They liked rice and bread. They even liked apples, grapes and bananas. But they did not like vegetables.

One day, their mom told them a story. Long ago, the Native people in Canada grew three special vegetables. They planted corn, beans and pumpkins very close to each other in the garden.

The corn grew strong and tall. The beans climbed up the big strong corn stems. The pumpkins made big leaves as they grew. The leaves kept the ground cool and wet.

The three vegetables helped each other. They were like three sisters in a family.

That is why the Native people call these vegetables the three sisters. They are very special. Little kids grow big and strong by eating corn, beans and pumpkins.

Now, Eddy and Casey eat their vegetables every day.

21

Baseball or Piano?

My mom loves music. She wants me to become a pianist. But I like sports. I play baseball every day after school. Sometimes, I stay out playing until it gets dark.

So when my mom signed me up for piano lessons, I was not happy. Mom said that I had to try the piano for one year.

I went to the first lesson. It was very difficult. My fingers were not good at pushing the right piano keys. They were good at holding a ball.

A little girl there saw me struggling. She said to me, "I will help you learn to play the piano if you teach me to play baseball."

We became good friends that day. She taught me how to play Beethoven. And I taught her to throw a curve ball.

Now, I don't know which I like better, baseball or piano?

22

The Missing Gloves

This year, my mom made me a new pair of gloves for my birthday. That day, I wore them to the skating rink.

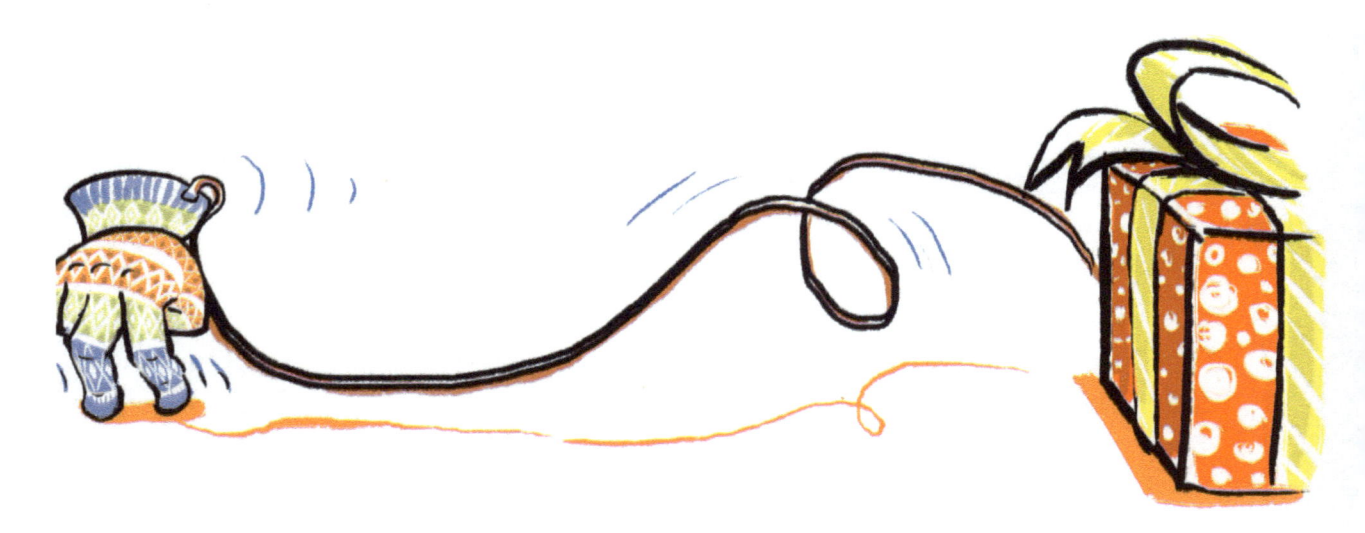

It got quite warm. Everyone took off their heavy coats and hats. I took off my new gloves. I put them safely in my jacket and skated around in my sweater.

When it was time to go home, I picked up my jacket. But my gloves were gone!

I could not believe it. I went home and told my parents. They were upset with me. I felt terrible.

Later that evening, the doorbell rang. It was a boy from school. He had the exact same jacket as me. I had accidentally picked up the wrong jacket!

"Missing these?" he asked as he handed me my gloves and jacket. I had never been so happy to see a pair of gloves in my whole life!

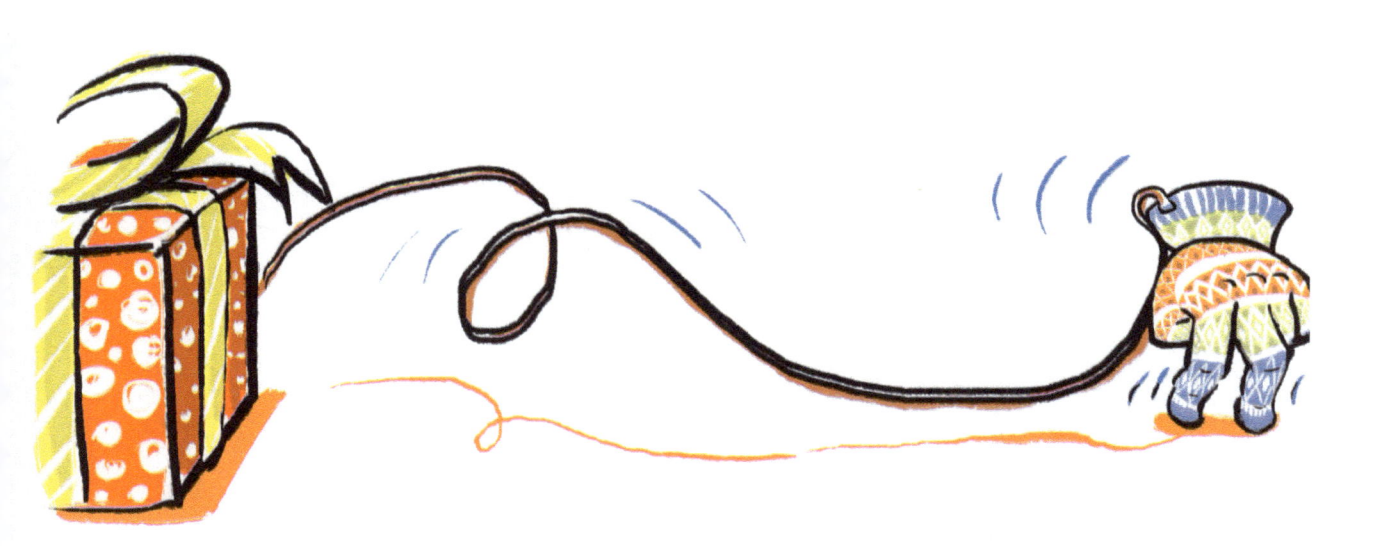

23

The Gentle Giant

You probably already know that elephants are the largest land animals.

Some people think that, next to humans, elephants are the smartest creatures on earth.

In some ways, they are just like us: they live in groups to be about the same age as a human. The oldest elephant was 82 years old.

Just how big can elephants get? Well, there was once a male elephant that weighed 11,000 kilograms. That's as much as ten cars!

Elephants have been known to knock down trees and carry them out of forests. There are even reports of elephants pushing trains off railway tracks.

But for all their size and strength, elephants can be very gentle. And any creature that's as big as a house deserves respect!

24

Protect Mom's Belly

Irene is four years old. She is very smart. She observes everything. Her mom is going to have a baby!

One day, her mom asked her, "Irene, do you want a baby sister? You are too lonely."

"No!" Irene replied.

"How about a baby brother?" Mom asked.

"No!" Irene replied again.

"Why? Wouldn't you like to have a sister or brother to play with?" Mom asked again.

"I would want to play with my sister or brother! But I just wouldn't want your belly to explode. You will feel so much pain. It's getting so big and round," Irene said.

Mom laughed, "Don't worry. My belly won't explode."

"Why don't we ask Dad to give birth to the baby? He is big and strong," Irene asked.

Dad started laughing too. "I'm a man and men can't do that."

25

How Old Are You?

One day, some friends were talking. They were talking about how old they were.

James said, "I am seven years old. My brother is older. He is twice as old as me. How old is my brother?"

"That's easy," said Ellen. "You are seven. He is twice as old as you. So, your brother is seven plus seven. He is fourteen years old."

Then Jane said, "I am eight. I have a baby sister. She is half my age. How old is my sister?"

"That's so easy!" yelled James. "She is half of eight. So, your sister is four years old."

Chris was thinking hard. There was something on his mind. Then, he asked, "How old is a dinosaur?"

"A dinosaur?!" said the puzzled children.

"Yes, how old is a dinosaur?" said Chris again.

The children thought really hard.

"A dinosaur is old—very old," said Ellen. "A dinosaur is millions of years old. A dinosaur is old, old, old!"

The children laughed. James said, "A dinosaur is older than all of us combined!"

26

Molly Can't Fall Asleep

Little Molly goes to bed, but she cannot fall asleep. She sits up. She lies down again. Still, she cannot sleep. It is not fun at all. Molly wants to sleep. What can she do?

Mommy teaches Molly a trick. It will help her fall asleep. It is fun and easy. What is it? Counting sheep! Close your eyes and try it.

Imagine a small wall—not too high and not too low—just right for sheep to jump over. Now imagine a flock of sheep. How many are there? Let's count them. Count the sheep as they jump over the wall.

One sheep, two sheep, three sheep, four...

Molly begins to count the sheep. *Ten, eleven, twelve...* Keep your eyes closed. Keep counting, Molly. Watch the sheep and count.

One hundred, one hundred and one, one hundred and two... Count, count, count. What's that sound? It's the sound of Molly sleeping.

27

Working with Dad

One Saturday morning, my dad got me up early and said to me, "Can you help me in the workshop today?"

"Sure!" I said. I was always willing to help Dad in his workshop. But he never asked me. I thought it was because I am a girl. But today was different. He actually asked for my help!

My dad had a drawing of his plans. We followed the plans and cut some wood. Soon, all the pieces were the right size and length.

We started to put the pieces together. It was a chair! We glued the pieces and used big clamps to hold them in place. Dad said we had to wait 24 hours for the glue to dry.

The next day, we went downstairs. "Go ahead," my dad said.

I sat down. It didn't fall apart!

I hope I will have a daughter one day. I will teach her how to make her own chair too.

28 What to Be

Our teacher asked us to write a paper. "I want everyone to write a paper for me," said the teacher. "In the paper, tell me what you want to be when you grow up."

"I want to work in a store and sell things," said Bill.

"I want to coach a baseball team," cried Sam.

"I want to be a writer and write books for people to read," said Cheryl.

"I want to be a fireman," said Gerry. "And maybe a policeman too."

All of the children were excited—all except Joey.

"I can't make up my mind," he said.

"I want to be a lot of different things."

The teacher smiled. "Then that's what you should write," she told him.

"Write about all the things you want to be. One day, you'll know which one to choose. For right now, wanting to be a lot of things is just right."

29

Big Green Ball

Sean had a new green ball—the best ball in the world! He took the ball into the garden. He rolled, bounced and kicked it. It was a great ball!

His little brother Sam wanted the ball too. "No!" said Sean. "It's my ball! ALL MINE!"

Sean kicked the ball hard. It flew high, high in the sky and over the fence!

The fence was very tall, much taller than Sean. There was also a hole in the fence. It was much smaller than Sean.

Sean started to cry because he couldn't get his ball back.

But, Sam was small. He said, "Let me go get it." He crawled through the hole and reached for the ball. Then he came back.

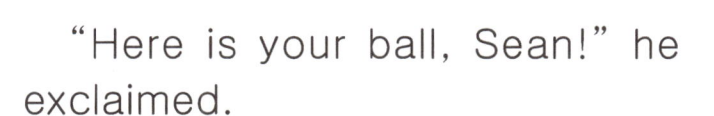

"Here is your ball, Sean!" he exclaimed.

Sean looked at Sam and smiled. "No, it's OUR ball!"

Kenny's Adventure

Kenny was going on an adventure. Where was he going? He was going to the grocery store!

He was going to get some groceries, all by himself.

Kenny's mom gave him a list and some money. "You need to get bread, milk and butter," she told him. "And be sure to use the crosswalk and to look both ways when crossing the street."

Kenny walked to the crosswalk. He looked both ways carefully. Then, he looked again, just to be sure there were no cars coming. Finally, he crossed the street and went into the store.

Kenny gave the grocery list to the clerk. "I want bread, milk and butter," he told the clerk. "Here is the money."

The clerk put the things in a bag and handed it to Kenny, with some change. Kenny was excited!

He walked back safely and made his way home. He had had a wonderful adventure!

31

Baby Brother

Little Mary lives in a big house with her parents. She is the only child in the family. She really wants to have a baby brother.

One day, when she comes home from school, Mom and Dad are waiting for her. "We have some good news," they say. "You will have a baby brother soon."

Mary is very, very happy. "Is this true? When will he be here?" she asks. "I can't wait for him."

Her father says, "We will get him in two weeks."

"Two weeks?" asks Mary. "Doesn't it take longer than that for a baby?"

Mom smiles at Mary. "We are going to adopt a baby boy," she explains. "That means that we are going to choose a baby who has no family. We will be his new family. We will take care of him."

Mary is so excited. She will be a big sister in just two weeks!

Scan the code to listen to the online audio.

One Story A Day

for Early Readers

(Book 2 for February)

DC Canada Education Publishing

Table of Contents

1. Getting a Pet 68
2. Running a Race 70
3. A Simple Man 72
4. A Little Good Luck 74
5. The Sky Is Falling 76
6. Get Some Air 78
7. The Barber Shop 80
8. The Same But Different 82
9. Gift of Hope 84
10. Panic 86
11. Living Things 88
12. Proud of My Past 90
13. Don't Cry, Mom 92
14. A Day to Say "I Like You!" 94
15. Getting Eyeglasses 96
16. Help the Whales 98

17	A Visit with Dr. Mom	100
18	A Star for My Birthday	102
19	Is My Sister a Foreigner?	104
20	Tomorrow	106
21	Friends	108
22	A Morning Surprise	110
23	Mr. Slow and Mr. Fast	112
24	Never Too Old to Travel	114
25	How We Got Night and Day	116
26	A Big Cat	118
27	A Painful Lesson	120
28	Reading to Grandchildren	122

1
Getting a Pet

Yan loves animals. He wants a pet. There is only one problem. His family lives in a very small apartment.

He begs his parents to let him have a puppy. But his father says, "A puppy is small. But puppies grow into big dogs. We have no space for a dog."

So, Yan asks for a kitten. His mom looks at her son. She wants him to have a pet. But the apartment is SO small.

"We cannot get a kitten either," she says. "Kittens become cats. And cats are big."

Yan is sad. But he understands.

Then one day, he comes home from school and sees something on his table.

It's a bowl filled with water. Inside is a pretty little goldfish! It is swimming around and around. Yan laughs with joy.

Now, Yan has a pet. He calls his goldfish Goldie. Goldie is his very best friend!

2

Running a Race

Every year, we have a race at school to see who can run the fastest. And every year, my friend Jim wins.

This year, I decided to work very hard to beat Jim. I trained very hard and ran every day.

Finally, the day of the race came.

Everyone got ready at the start line. Then, the gun went off with a "Bang!" I was in the lead, but I could tell Jim was catching up fast.

Soon, we were running together. It was the last turn before the finish line. We ran side by side. It was fun! We did not care who won anymore. We could always share the prize.

We were having so much fun that we did not notice that another boy had passed us both! Joey zipped by at the very last second.

In the end, Jim and I shared second place.

3
A Simple Man

Mahatma Gandhi was a simple man who did great things. He led his country to independence. And the way he did it was amazing!

He did not believe in violence. He did not believe in fighting or in wars. He believed in talking things out.

The Indian people agreed with him. In 1947, India became a free country.

Gandhi lived a poor life by choice. He was a well-educated lawyer. He earned a good salary. But he saw the poor people around him and decided to help them.

He learned how to live in the simplest way possible and still be healthy. He ate mostly fruit, goat's milk and olive oil. He wore only a simple rag as clothing. But people followed him. They could see that he was honest.

Gandhi spoke his native language. He also learned English. But he spoke English with an Irish accent. Why? His first English teacher was Irish!

4

A Little Good Luck

An old lady lives on our street. She is very rich. One day, I saw her bending down, trying to pick something up off the ground. She was having a hard time.

So, I came over and asked if I could help. She told me there was a penny on the ground. I wondered why a rich lady was worried about a penny.

"Oh, I don't need it," she said. "But it is good luck to find a penny!"

I gave her the penny and walked away. Just then, the old lady called me back. She put the coin in my shirt pocket and said, "It will bring you extra good luck because you helped me!"

At home, I pulled out the coin. I was surprised—she hadn't given me the penny. She had given me a dollar coin!

5
The Sky Is Falling

Chicken was resting under a tree when a nut fell and hit her on the head. She jumped up and yelled, "The sky is falling! The sky is falling!"

She started to run. "I must tell the king," she cried. "There is surely danger here."

On the way, Chicken met Duck. "The sky is falling!" she cried.

"How do you know?" asked Duck.

"I saw it! A piece of it hit me on the head." And so, the two set off to warn the king.

They met Rabbit and Turtle on the way.

Chicken cried, "The sky is falling!" She said that she had seen it with her own eyes. Rabbit and Turtle were scared too. So they joined the race to warn the king.

Then, Fox showed up. "What is the matter?" he asked. When he heard the answer, he smiled and said, "You will never find the king unless I show you the way. Follow me."

The animals followed Fox into his home. All of a sudden, he locked the door and wanted to eat them all up!

6

Get Some Air

You do it all the time. If you stopped doing it, you would be in trouble. What is it? It's breathing!

Everyone needs air. We breathe without even thinking about it. It's automatic.

But how do we do it? Put your hand on your chest. Take a deep breath of air. Do you feel your chest getting bigger? Now let the air out. Feel how small it gets.

Inside your chest are two large sacks. They are like big balloons. They are your lungs.

When you breathe in, your lungs fill up with air. Breathe out, and the air goes out too.

Most people take 22,000 breaths of air each day! Your lungs work really hard. That's why you should take good care of your lungs. Do not smoke. Get exercise and breathe deeply.

One more thing... when you yawn, it means you're not getting enough air. Your lungs are telling you to take another big breath.

7 The Barber Shop

Jimmy is crying. He doesn't want to get his hair cut. He is afraid.

It is his first time going to a barber. He does not like the sounds in a barber shop. There are many strange smells too.

Mr. Howard, the barber, smiles. "Hello Jimmy," he says. "So, this is your first haircut? I will take good care of you."

He begins to cut. Jimmy closes his eyes. "Please don't cut my ear!" he cries.

As he works, the barber talks to Jimmy. "Do you know that people who have red hair like you have only 90,000 hairs on their head? People who have black hair have more than 110,000 hairs."

"Hmmm, that is interesting," thinks Jimmy.

"The average hair lives about five and a half years. And we lose about 100 hairs a day," says Mr. Howard.

Jimmy likes the barber. In no time at all, the barber says, "You can open your eyes now." Jimmy cannot believe it. It didn't hurt. It was fun. And, he learned something interesting about hair.

8

The Same but Different

Becky and Sherry are twins. Becky loves dresses. Her sister Sherry loves sports.

One day, their mother said to them, "Let's buy some new clothes for you." So they went to the store together.

Their mother chose some very nice dresses for them. Becky was happy. But Sherry was not.

"How can I play baseball in this?" she asked.

Sherry looked at a boy who was trying on a pair of shorts. Sherry's mom saw this. "Well," she said. "Would you like some shorts instead?"

Sherry was very happy. "That would be great!" she said.

"All right. I will buy a dress for Becky and shorts for Sherry," Mom said.

"Sometimes I forget that although you two look the same, it doesn't mean you ARE the same," laughed their mother.

9 Gift of Hope

My mom always gives money to charities. We get more and more calls to our home. Letters are sent to Mom, all of them with good reasons to ask for donations.

But Mom does not have enough money to meet all her urges to give. She has to consider her choices carefully.

One day, Mom received a letter with the title Gift of Hope.

The letter said, "It's not money. It's hope. It's the gift of hope for families in poor countries."

Mom continued reading the letter. "With $19, you can give three hens to a family.

The hens will lay eggs, which the family can then sell. With this money, the family can pay for their basic needs."

Mom smiled as she read. She made a plan to save money and send to this charity regularly.

10 Panic

It's always fun to learn about words. Sometimes, if we know where a word comes from, it is easier to understand its meaning. Take the word panic, for example.

This popular English word comes from the Greek language. Many English words are based on this ancient language.

Pan was the Greek god of shepherds. He was half man, half animal. He liked to hunt and play music. He liked to walk through the woods, playing his special flute.

He often frightened people with his strange appearance. When people met him, they were so fearful that they did not know what to do. They were in a panic.

This is the origin of the word panic. A person in a panic is frightened and confused. Often, people in a panic do foolish things.

11
Living Things

A flower is a living thing. A tree is a living thing. Grass is a living thing too.

You are a living thing. I am a living thing. Bees, birds, dogs and cats—these are all living things.

What is a living thing? It is something that is alive. It starts out small. But it grows big and strong. The world is filled with many living things.

All living things need food and water to grow.

Think about yourself. When you are hungry, you need to eat. When a tree is hungry, it needs to eat too. You eat fruit and vegetables. You eat meat and fish. But a tree gets its food from things in the ground.

You drink water when you are thirsty. A flower drinks water too. A tree gets its water from the ground.

Take a look at all living things. We are the same. But we are all different too.

12 Proud of My Past

My name is Leo. My family is from the Ojibway tribe. At first, I didn't think this was special. But that was before I learned how interesting my people are!

We lived in North America long before anyone else. Some people think we might have come from Asia thousands of years ago.

In those days, my people lived off the land. We never did anything that would cause pollution. We respected the earth. We respected each other.

We never wasted anything either. The water, the trees, and the land were very special to us.

Today, the whole world thinks about these things. But we have always been like this.

I am proud of the history of the Native people. I am also proud to be a Canadian.

13

Don't Cry, Mom

One day, when I walked into the kitchen, I saw my mom crying. "Mommy, what happened? Why are you sad?" I asked.

Mom smiled at me. "I have tears in my eyes," she said. "But I am not sad."

"I am cutting onions, as you can see," Mom said.

"Onions have a strong chemical that hurts our eyes. But don't worry. Our body is amazing. It senses the danger of this chemical and sends tears to our eyes to get rid of it. Tears protect our eyes from danger."

That is interesting! I learned something else too. All animals cry to protect their eyes. But humans are the only animals that cry when they are sad.

I love learning about my body. It all seems to work perfectly! The more I learn about it, the more amazed I am.

A Day to Say "I Like You!"

Every year, on February 14, people around the world say, "I like you!" in a special way.

They send or give a card to a person they really like. The day is called Valentine's Day. It is very popular in the United States, Canada and England.

In many schools, kids spend part of Valentine's Day making cards. They give them to friends, teachers and special people.

No one knows for sure why this special day began. It takes its name from a Christian saint, called Saint Valentine. But not much is known about him.

It's always a good thing to stop and tell someone how much you like them on any day of the year. But it's kind of nice to know that on February 14, millions of people are doing the same thing you are.

15 Getting Eyeglasses

Little Freddie was having trouble in school. His mom was worried. So she took Freddie to see a doctor.

Dr. Adams gave him an eye test. He told Freddie that he did not see as well as the other kids.

"Your eyes are weak," said Dr. Adams.
"You have trouble seeing what the teacher writes on the board. That's why you need to get eyeglasses."

"Oh no!" Freddie cried. "I don't want to wear glasses. The kids will make fun of me." His mom said, "Don't you want to do better in school?"

The doctor said, "You have a problem with your eyesight. Wearing glasses will help prevent it from getting worse.

Some people can even go blind if they don't take care of this problem. I'm sure your friends will understand."

That night, Freddie decided that it was better to wear glasses than to grow up and become blind.

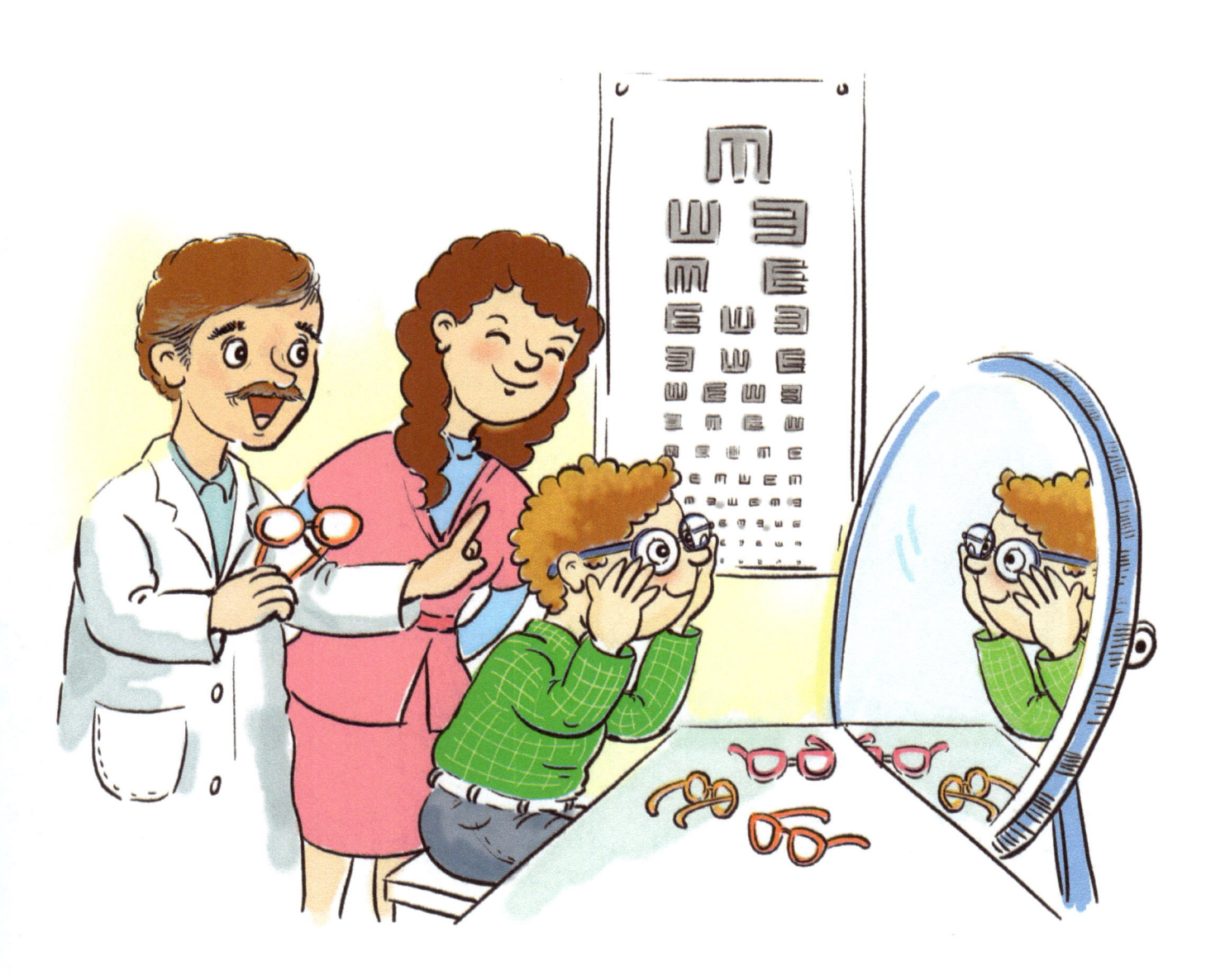

97

16
Help the Whales

Whales are big animals—really BIG! Some whales are bigger than elephants. One kind of whale is actually the biggest animal in the world.

Whales swim in water. Fish swim in water too. But whales are not fish. Fish can breathe under water. But, whales have to come up to the surface of the water to breathe.

Whales can talk to each other. They have a special language. People cannot understand whale talk. But whales understand each other.

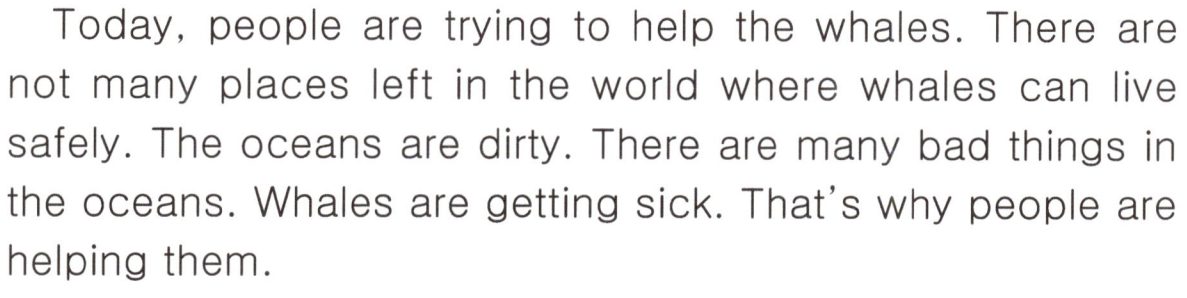

Today, people are trying to help the whales. There are not many places left in the world where whales can live safely. The oceans are dirty. There are many bad things in the oceans. Whales are getting sick. That's why people are helping them.

What can you do to help the whales? Tell people how special whales are. Tell people not to put garbage in the oceans.

17

A Visit with Dr. Mom

Emmy dropped her teddy bear in the yard. "Oh, his leg is broken," cried Emmy.

"I think you need a doctor," Emmy told him. The teddy bear seemed scared. He stared at Emmy.

"Don't worry," Emmy said. "I'll take you to Dr. Mom. It won't hurt a bit."

Emmy told the teddy bear what would happen. "First, we'll go inside. Then, we'll read stories while we wait for Dr. Mom to see us. When Dr. Mom is ready, she'll look at your leg and fix it."

Emmy told him that she would hold his hand. He wasn't scared anymore.

So, Emmy carried her teddy bear inside. Then she read him a story.

Finally, Dr. Mom was ready to see them. She fixed the teddy bear's leg and said, "He's as good as new now."

Emmy gave her teddy bear a big hug. He was brave while Dr. Mom fixed his leg!

18 A Star for My Birthday

It was my birthday. My whole family went horseback riding. It's easy for us because we live on a farm in the countryside.

That night, we sat around a campfire and looked at the stars.

My mother brought out a cake with candles on it. "Make a wish," she said. I wished for my own horse.

Just as I blew out the candle, a bright light filled the sky. It was a shooting star. It soared across the sky.

My mom said a shooting star is a very small rock. It moves so fast that it makes the air around it catch fire.

I'm sure she's right, but I think it's a sign that my wish will come true. If it does, I think I'll name my horse *Star*.

103

19

Is My Sister a Foreigner?

Erin lives with her parents in Canada. Both of her parents are Chinese. But Erin was born in Canada. Her friends in kindergarten are different colours.

One day, Mom said to her, "Erin, you will have a baby sister very soon."

Erin was very happy. She thought for a little while, then asked, "Mom, is my sister going to be Chinese or a foreigner? Will her eyes be black or blue? And what about her hair? What colour will it be? Will it be black or brown?"

Mom laughed, "Your dad and mom are Chinese, so you will have a baby sister just like you."

Erin smiled. She walked away thinking of all the fun she was going to have with her new baby sister.

20 Tomorrow

There once was a man who was very lazy. Every day, a farmer would tell the man, "If you help me bring in my crops, I will give you food." But the lazy man would always answer, "Maybe tomorrow."

The summer turned to winter. One day, the lazy man did not have any food left. So, he went to the farmer and knocked on his door. He asked, "Can I work for some food today?"

The farmer said, "I'm sorry, there's no more work to be done." The man walked away. He sat by the side of the road. He was really hungry.

Later, the farmer came up to him and said, "If you help me cut wood, I'll give you some food."

Then, the farmer smiled and said, "Or would you like to wait until tomorrow?"

The man jumped up and started to work immediately.

21

Friends

One day, Turtle lost his footing and rolled down a riverbank. He landed belly-up on his shell. The riverbank was very muddy and Turtle was stuck.

"Help! Help!" called Turtle.

Cat came strolling by. "What's wrong?" asked the cat.

"I'm stuck. Can you roll me over?" asked Turtle.

Cat pushed Turtle over onto his belly. Turtle swam away and said, "Thanks Cat. I'll remember this!"

Not long after, Cat was chasing a squirrel on a tree. Snap! The tree branch cracked and fell. Cat landed on a large rock in the middle of the river.

"Help! Help!" called Cat. Turtle came swimming by. "What's wrong?" asked Turtle.

"I can't swim. Can you carry me to land?" asked Cat.

"Sure," said Turtle. "Climb onto my back."

Cat rode to safety on the back of her new friend, Turtle.

22 A Morning Surprise

There are many kinds of hair. There is long hair and short hair. There is straight hair and curly hair. Some people have black or brown hair. Other people have red or blonde hair.

Some people lose their hair when they get old. Other people's hair turns grey. It usually takes many years for a person's hair to turn grey.

But something strange happened to my father. His hair was black when he went to bed. By morning, it had turned completely grey! Why?

Dad had been feeling very stressed lately. He had lost his job. He was worried about his family. He was worried about paying the bills. He was worried about feeding us. He was worrying all the time.

The doctor said that what happened to my dad does not happen often. But it does happen. Worry and stress are very bad. They can turn hair grey overnight!

23 Mr. Slow and Mr. Fast

Mr. Slow and Mr. Fast are friends. But they are not the same.

Mr. Slow always takes his time. He talks slowly. He walks slowly. He even takes a long time to eat. Mr. Slow is really slow.

Mr. Fast is the opposite. He is always in a hurry. He talks fast. He walks fast. He even rushes when he eats. Mr. Fast is really fast.

One day, the two men went to a restaurant. As usual, Mr. Fast ordered his food right away. Mr. Slow took a long time to decide what he wanted. Mr. Fast finished eating before Mr. Slow even got his meal.

Still, Mr. Fast waited for his friend. "Take your time," he said quickly. "You are slow, like a turtle. I am fast, like a rabbit. But I can wait because you are my friend."

113

24

Never Too Old to Travel

My grandma was coming for a visit on her birthday. What was so special about that? Grandma was turning 100 years old! But even more amazing—she was travelling by airplane.

Mom said flying was not easy. What if Grandma got lost at the airport? What if she got sick on the plane? Many things could go wrong.

We were nervous. We went to the airport early.

Then we saw her. Grandma was with the pilot. He was smiling. Grandma waved. I ran to give her a hug.

The pilot said, "When I heard she was coming to celebrate her 100th birthday, I knew how lucky I was. She is the oldest passenger I have ever had fly on my plane."

I gave Grandma a big kiss. She smiled and said, "On my 101st birthday, maybe I will dive in the ocean." We all laughed. Grandma is not afraid of anything.

25

How We Got Night and Day

(based on a Native American legend)

Long ago, the world was new. It was fresh and clean. Everyone agreed on everything.

Then, the animals began to argue. Some of them wanted it to be night all the time. Others wanted it to be day all the time.

They asked Bear to make the decision for them. Bear liked the night. "Let's have night all the time," he said.

But Squirrel jumped up and said, "Look at Racoon. See the rings on his tail? One is dark, then light, then dark again. The number of dark rings is the same as the number of light rings. I say we have equal parts night and day."

The animals were impressed. They saw the wisdom in this.

And that is how we came to have day and night.

26

A Big Cat

The average cat weighs about five or six kilograms. And most cats like to catch mice.

But there is one cat who doesn't bother with mice.

His name is Hercules. You see, Hercules weighs over 400 kilograms. He is two metres tall and three metres long! He prefers to eat much bigger things than mice.

He is the biggest cat in the world. Hercules was born in a zoo. His father was a lion and his mother was a tiger. He is called a Liger.

You would think that something so big must not be able to move very fast. How can he?

But Hercules can run at 90 kilometres per hour.

And he needs this exercise because he eats 100 pounds of food for every meal!

That would be a lot of mice!

27

A Painful Lesson

Becky loves to win. She wants to be the first in everything.

One day we were out biking. Becky was in front. It bothered me that my friend always had to be in charge.

I felt angry. I started to pedal faster and I passed her. Soon, she passed me again.

When we reached a corner, I ran right into Becky. We both went flying and landed on the grass. I hurt my knee and Becky's elbow was badly bruised.

Our parents took us to the hospital. I felt terrible. "I wanted to win so much that I cut across the lawn and we collided," I said.

"It's my fault," Becky said. "Instead of letting you pass, I had to win. I'm sorry."

I gave my best friend a hug. We had both grown up a little that day. But it was a painful lesson.

28

Reading to Grandchildren

Mr. Than is seventy years old. He lives in a village in Vietnam. He worked hard all his life as a rice farmer. But now, he is retired. He spends his days enjoying his old age.

There is one thing you should know about Mr. Than.

Mr. Than never went to school. When he was a boy, he had to go to work. Now, Mr. Than has a dream. He wants to learn to read. He wants to read to his grandchildren.

Last year, a new teacher came to the school in his

village. The teacher opened a night class to teach adults to read. Of course, Mr. Than signed up right away. Now, he goes to school two nights a week.

It is not easy. But already, he can read more than 500 words. Mr. Than is dreaming about the day he will be able to read to his grandchildren. It makes him very happy to think about it.

Scan the code to listen to the audio online.

One Story A Day

for Early Readers

(Book 3 for March)

DC Canada Education Publishing

Table of Contents

1	First Flower in Spring	128
2	A Day of Fishing	130
3	Danger: Thin Ice	132
4	Afraid of Wind	134
5	Our Amazing Eyes	136
6	Where Is the Money From?	138
7	Our Friendly Sun	140
8	Brush Twice a Day (I)	142
9	Brush Twice a Day (II)	144
10	Butterflies and Bird Song	146
11	The Judge	148
12	Gold or Corn?	150
13	Seashells	152
14	Our Little Friend	154
15	Chicken Eggs	156
16	Why Is It Colder Up There?	158

17	The Mouse in the House	160
18	Mean Mr. Green	162
19	My Older Brother	164
20	Tommy's Box	166
21	A Family Picture	168
22	Tears in the Ocean	170
23	For the Love of Kids	172
24	What Is Under the Bed?	174
25	Two Friends	176
26	Happy to Be Busy	178
27	What Colour Is That?	180
28	Old Dog, New Tricks	182
29	The Little Seeds	184
30	Snowflakes	186
31	Grandma, the Biker	188

1

First Flower in Spring

Outside our kitchen window, there is a tree. No one in our family knew what kind of tree it was when we first moved in.

Early that spring, the tree started to grow little buds and yellow petals. But there was still snow on the ground!

At first, I thought the yellow buds were the leaves of the tree. My sister agreed and guessed, "It must be the cold weather that made the tree leaves yellow, instead of green."

But a few weeks later, green leaves began to appear on the tree branches along with the yellow petals! We then realized that the yellow "leaves" that appeared first were actually flowers!

This was the first time we saw a tree bear flowers before leaves. The discovery made us all very excited!

Mom and Dad borrowed a book from the library. Together, we learned about this flowering plant. It is called *forsythia*. To us, it's the first sign of spring.

2

A Day of Fishing

Little Henry really likes fishing. He and his dad spend a lot of time fishing on the river.

Most times, Henry catches fish and throws them back into the river. Sometimes, he has a competition with Dad to see who can catch the biggest fish.

It is Saturday again. Henry sits on the riverbank for almost an hour. Still, no fish bite. His dad smiles and says, "Fishing is a sport. It exercises your patience."

No problem. Henry loves fishing, even when he is not catching fish. He enjoys the river. He loves watching the birds on the water.

Suddenly, Henry feels something. He feels a tug at the end of the fishing rod.

"Dad, it's a big one!" Henry cries. His dad comes to help. Henry pulls and pulls. In his mind, he imagines a HUGE fish.

Finally, he brings it out of the water. But, it is not a fish. It's a turtle!

3

Danger: Thin Ice

Alice and her dad walk beside the river. They are taking their dog Snoopy for a walk. It is a beautiful day in early March. The sun is high and warm. There are no clouds in the sky.

All of a sudden, Snoopy sees something on the ice. He runs to catch it. Alice shouts, "NO! Stop, Snoopy!" But it is too late. The ice breaks and Snoopy falls into the cold water.

Alice runs to help her dog. But Dad stops her. "Do not go on the ice," he says. Then, he calls 911. Soon, the firefighters arrive. They crawl on a ladder over the ice to save the little dog.

When they bring it back to shore, Alice cries. She is so happy! The fireman says, "You were smart. Never go on the ice to save your dog. It is too dangerous. Do not trust the ice in late winter. Always call for help."

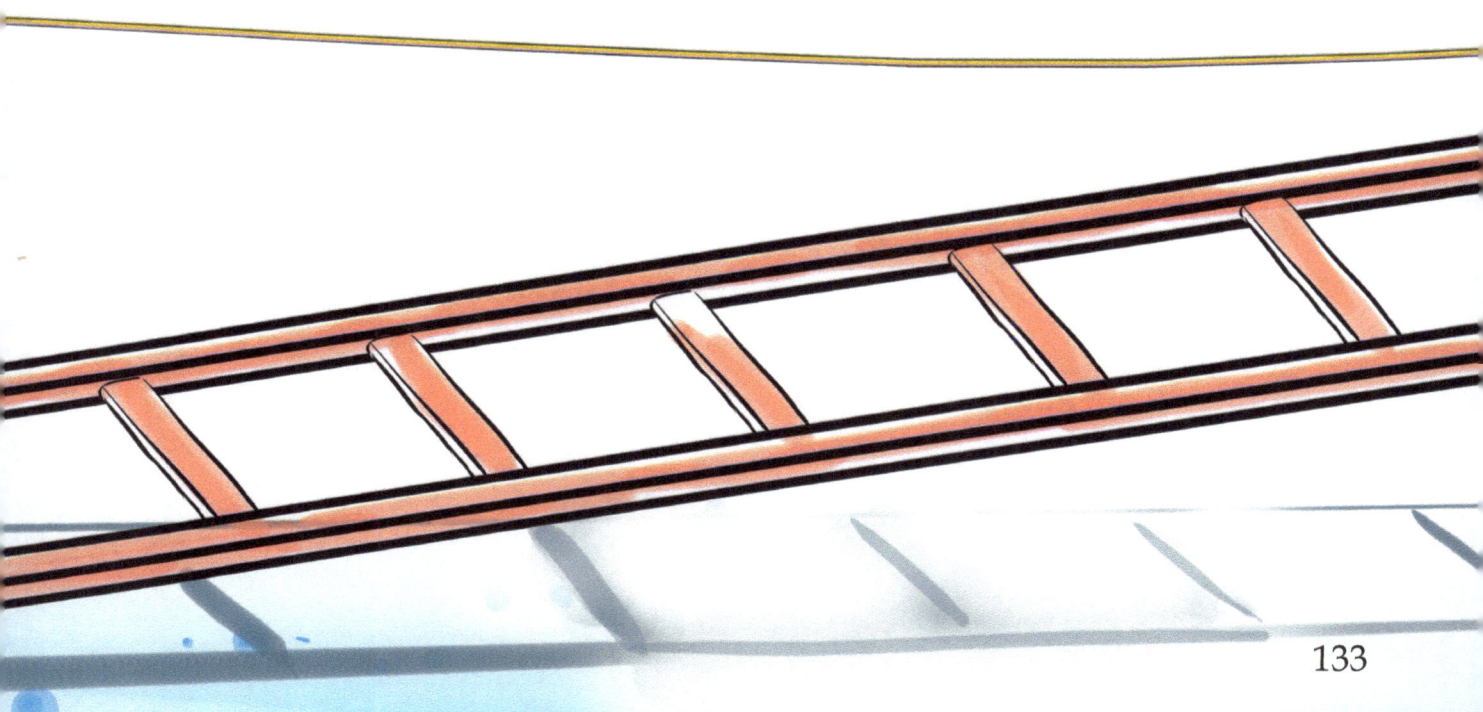

4

Afraid of Wind

When I was a little girl, I was afraid of the wind. It made lots of noises and made everyone feel cold. "I don't like wind," I told my father. Father smiled.

One day, as the wind was blowing strongly, I cried "Look at the trees. They are all bent. I think it's trees that cause wind. Let's cut down all the trees. Then there will be no more wind!"

Father laughed. He told me that trees don't create wind. Instead, trees slow down the wind.

"But where does the wind come from?" I asked.

"It comes from the air—moving air is wind. Air and wind are part of the natural world," explained my father. "Without wind, the hot areas would be too hot, and the cold areas would be too cold. It would be a big problem for our world."

I still get nervous when a strong wind blows. But I always remember the way my father took the time to explain it to me.

5

Our Amazing Eyes

Today in school, we learned something amazing. Nearly 2,500 people in Canada go blind each year because they injure their eyes.

Our eyes weigh only 28 grams. But they are really important. Imagine what it would be like if you could not see.

Luckily, our bodies are designed to protect our eyes.

Our eyebrows keep salty sweat from running into our eyes. Our eyelashes keep dirt from getting into our eyes. And tears wash away any dirt that gets past our eyelashes.

Want to hear something amazing? We blink our eyes 10 million times a year! Each time we blink, a little water enters our eyes and washes dust and dirt away.

Did you know that you cannot sneeze with your eyes open? It's true.

Next time you feel a sneeze coming, see if you can keep your eyes open while you sneeze. You won't be able to!

6

Where Is the Money From?

Irene doesn't like it when her mother goes to work.

Every day, she begs her mom to stay home. "Can you please stay home? Can you pick me up from school? Pleeease, Mom!"

But, her mother always says, "No, honey! I need to work." Irene doesn't understand. "Why?" she asks.

Mom explains it to her, "We need money to pay for our food, house, car, books and toys. I go to work to make money for us."

Irene quickly replies, "No, Mom. When you need money, you just go to the bank to get it." Then she adds, "I saw that the other day."

Mom laughs and says, "Yes, I can go to the bank to get money. But that's only possible once I have earned the money and put it in a bank account."

7
Our Friendly Sun

Look up. Look at the sky. But do not look at the sun. The sun is very strong. Its light is so powerful that it can hurt your eyes.

Do you know how far the sun is from the earth? It's about 150 million kilometres away! Wow! That's really far.

Even though the sun is far away, the light is still very strong when it reaches us. So, the sun is one of the most powerful things in our world.

Do not be afraid of the sun. It is an important friend. It keeps us warm. It gives us light so we can see. It makes flowers and trees grow.

There can be no life on earth without the sun. That is why we call it our friendly sun. It is our friend because it gives us many things.

But be careful. It is a very powerful friend.

8

Brush Twice a Day (I)

There is one thing that I really, really HATE doing. What is it? Brushing my teeth. I just don't see the reason for all this brushing.

Mom is always making sure I brush in the morning, and I brush my teeth before bed too. WHY? That's what I want to know.

Mom is a science teacher. She likes experiments. She says, "Showing is always better than telling." So, we make a deal.

First, Mom has to prove that it is really important to brush teeth at least twice a day. If she does, I will brush my teeth without any complaining.

"Okay," says Mom. "Here is what we need for this experiment. We need a boiled egg. We need a small jar. We need some vinegar."

Vinegar is sour and really strong. I think this will be interesting. I can hardly wait to see what Mom is going to do!

9

Brush Twice a Day (II)

We boil the egg. When it has cooled, Mom hits the shell with a spoon. The shell doesn't break. It protects the inside of the egg,

She says, "Your teeth have a shell too. It is called *enamel*."

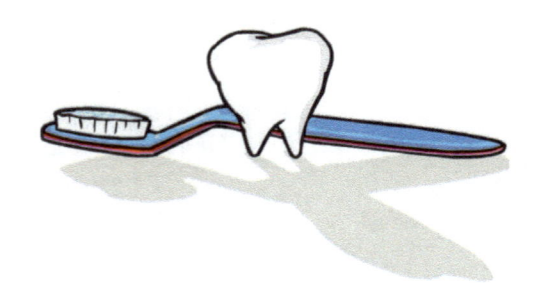

Now the fun part.

We fill the jar with vinegar. Then we put the egg inside and close the jar with a lid. Now, we wait.

What will happen? It is exciting. Two days later, we open the jar. The egg shell has become really soft. It is breaking into small pieces. Wow! What is that about?

"The vinegar is a strong acid, just like many foods we eat," Mom says. "The vinegar softens the egg shell so it cannot protect what is inside anymore."

Mom smiles at me and says, "That is why you must brush your teeth. Brushing cleans the acid off from them. If you do not brush, the acid will break the enamel. You will have many cavities and toothaches after."

"No, I don't want that!" I reply quickly.

My mother is smart. Now I know why I should brush my teeth.

10

Butterflies and Bird Song

(based on a Native American legend)

One day in late summer, a magic man was passing through a village. It was a wonderful, sunny day.

"Soon, it will be winter," thought the man. "It will be cold and grey. Everyone will be sad."

But, the man had a plan.

He gathered all the beautiful things of the world and put them into a magic bag. He collected a golden ray of sunshine, the green from the leaves of trees, the rich blue of the summer sky, and the flowers of many colours.

He heard the birds singing, so he added all their wonderful songs to the bag too.

Then, when he opened the bag, out flew the most beautiful creatures the world had ever seen—butterflies!

The birds agreed that the butterflies were beautiful. They would help the people remember the beauty of the world, even during the dark, cold winters.

But the birds asked the man to give them back their songs. "These belong to us," they cried. "Butterflies are still beautiful without our songs." The man agreed.

And so, from that time on, butterflies were silent and beautiful.

The Judge

Mr. Judge is a really nice man. Everyone likes him and respects his honesty. But he is not really a "judge". You know, the person who makes decisions in a court of law. That's a judge.

One day, my mother wanted to make a deal with a company from another country. But it was too late to get a lawyer. They wanted to write out the agreement by hand and sign it that day.

They asked Mr. Judge to write out the papers.

Right away, Mr. Judge put on his glasses. He sat at a big desk. He put the words on paper and read them clearly and loudly, just like a real judge.

Then everyone signed the agreement.

Mom says that it's interesting when people's jobs match their names.

Yes, I'd like to see Ms. Baker bake at the bakery.

12

Gold or Corn?

One day, a very hungry rooster was searching for food.

He was having no luck. It was getting late. But, no matter how hard he scratched the ground, the rooster could not find anything to eat.

Soon, the rooster struck something with his feet. "What is this?" he wondered. "Please let it be food. I really MUST eat, or I shall die."

He scratched again quickly, eager to uncover what was hidden in the ground. To his disappointment, he found a piece of gold.

The rooster stood sadly, looking at the big piece of shiny gold. What good is gold to a rooster? If a human finds gold, he sells it for a fortune. But a rooster cannot do anything with it.

The rooster walked away thinking, "Gold has no value to me. I would trade all the gold in a king's castle for one small kernel of corn."

13 Seashells

Do you like seashells? Do you enjoy walking on the beach and collecting seashells? I do.

Recently, my parents took me down south over the Christmas holidays. We had a wonderful time on a small southern island.

When we left Canada, the temperature was −20°C. When we landed at the airport on the island, it was +30°C.

Yes! We had leaped from winter to summer in just five hours!

After we checked in at our hotel, we all ran to see the ocean. AMAZING!

The waves were racing one after another towards the shore. As the water drew away, it left in front of us beautiful shells—shells in various shapes, colours and sizes.

I bent down to pick some up. Soon we had a pile of seashells on the beach.

Looking at the seashells, my dad said that each shell showed us a life in the ocean. Imagine how much life there is under the ocean surface!

14

Our Little Friend

It was late fall. We were eating dinner. Suddenly, we heard a loud BANG! A little bird flew right to the window, then fell to the ground.

154

We ran outside and saw that it was a baby crow. It was alive but one wing was not moving. It could not fly.

My dad picked up the bird. We put it in a box for the night. That one night turned into many nights.

We named the bird **Max**. Max became very friendly to us. He took food from our hands. After a few weeks, his wing healed. Then one day, he flew away.

Now, every time I see a crow, I wonder, "Is that Max?" Maybe he will come back for a visit one day.

15 Chicken Eggs

You find them on the ground, in trees and even in special houses built just for them. Their mother sits on them for weeks, but she does not hurt them. She just keeps them warm. Their parents have wings, and they will too.

Their most common colours are white and brown. They can be big, small or in between. Be careful. Some are very soft and can break easily.

What are they? Eggs, of course!

All around the world, people eat eggs. But chicken eggs are the most popular. Boiled or fried, they taste really good.

The Chinese are world leaders in chicken egg production, producing nearly 160 billion eggs a year.

Here's a challenge: one chicken can lay about 250 eggs in one year. That's a lot of eggs. Can you figure out how many chickens it will take to lay 160 billion eggs?

16

Why Is It Colder Up There?

Miso and his father are flying from Korea to Canada. Miso is very excited.

On the back of the seat, there is a small computer screen. It shows the path the jet is taking and how fast it is travelling. It also shows the temperature outside.

Miso notices something really strange. The temperature outside the jet is −55°C. That's really cold.

"When we left Seoul it was nearly +25°C," thinks Miso. "How can this be?"

So he asks his father a question. "In this jet, we are closer to the sun. Shouldn't it be much hotter because we are closer to the sun? Why is it colder up here?"

Father smiles. "The ground is very good at taking in the heat from the sun," he explains. "The sun heats up the ground, which then slowly lets go of the heat. But we are many miles above the ground now in this jet. The heat from the ground cannot reach us here."

Miso has learned something interesting today.

The Mouse in the House

One morning, Becky's father said, "There is a mouse in the kitchen. It is eating our food. We must get rid of it."

Becky felt sorry for the mouse. "What will you do? Will you kill the mouse?" she asked.

"No," replied her father. "We will set a special trap. When the mouse goes inside, it will not be able to get back out.

Then, we will take it to a field. It can live there with other mice."

That made Becky happy. The next day she looked at the mouse trap. There was a little grey mouse inside. It looked very frightened.

Becky and her father took the mouse to a big field. Her father put the trap on the ground. The mouse ran into the field.

18

Mean Mr. Green

"Hi Mr. Green!" Sally waved to the old man sitting on his front porch.

"Don't say hi to him. He's mean," whispered her friend, Josh.

"He's not mean. He's just sad.

"Sad about what?"

"His wife went away. That made him sad."

That night, Sally decided to draw a picture for her neighbour. She drew herself and Mr. Green sitting on his porch, drinking lemonade. She drew big smiles on their faces and a bright sun in the sky.

The next day, Sally gave Mr. Green the picture. He looked like he was going to cry. Sally felt bad.

"I just wanted to see you smile again," she said shyly.

Mr. Green looked up from the picture. "Would you like some lemonade, Sally?" he asked.

"Yes, I would. Thank you."

As Sally and Mr. Green sat on his porch enjoying their lemonade, mean Mr. Green was smiling again.

My Older Brother

My brother is the oldest among the six children in our family. He is smart, but he had to drop out of school at the age of twelve to help our parents—there were too many mouths to feed.

Late fall was the season for harvesting. My brother took me to the field where the sweet potatoes had just been harvested. We got up early to look for any sweet potatoes that had been left in the field.

With a heavy shovel, my brother started digging. My job was to watch the ground to see if any sweet potatoes appeared.

It was still a little dark. My eyes opened wide while my brother dug in the soil.

"Wait! I saw one!" I yelled. My brother stopped digging. I picked up the sweet potato and put it in a basket. We were so happy. We felt like we had found a gold mine!

An hour later, when other people had come to the field, our basket was filled with sweet potatoes.

20

Tommy's Box

Tommy had a magic box. It wasn't too big, and it wasn't too small. It was just the right size—perfect for Tommy to climb in and sit down.

When Tommy sat in his box, the box became whatever Tommy wanted it to be. Sometimes, it was a car and Tommy would drive along the highway.

Sometimes, it was a boat and Tommy would go fishing to catch fish for his family's supper.

Sometimes, it was a plane and Tommy would fly high over the town.

And sometimes, it was a rocket ship and Tommy was a famous astronaut.

Tommy likes his magic box better than any of the toys his mom bought from the store. Don't you wish you had a magic box like Tommy's?

Well, you can! All you need is a box!

21

A Family Picture

Little Irene drew an interesting picture. The picture was of a mother and a daughter sitting at a table in front of a house.

Mom asked, "Who are they?"

"It's me and you," said the little girl.

Dad saw the picture. He wasn't very happy. He asked, "Where is the daddy? Why am I not in the picture?"

"Daddy is reading books inside the house. He is not playing with us."

What Irene said was true. Her dad was busy studying to become a doctor. He spent all his time reading books. He was so busy that he didn't have time to sit outside with them.

Irene's mom pointed out, "See? That's how your daughter will remember you. If you keep busy like this all the time, you won't be in any of her childhood pictures."

From that day on, Irene's dad started going out more often with his daughter and wife.

22

Tears in the Ocean

Bess was very upset. She hurt her arm in the backyard. She cried a lot. Her mom cleaned the cut and put a bandage on it.

Her aunt gave her a glass of water. "Bess, you know those tears running down your cheeks are falling to the ground?"

"Yes," said Bess.

"Those tears go into the ground. The rain takes them to the river. And the river flows into the sea. Then the hot sun makes the wet air from the sea rise up into the sky."

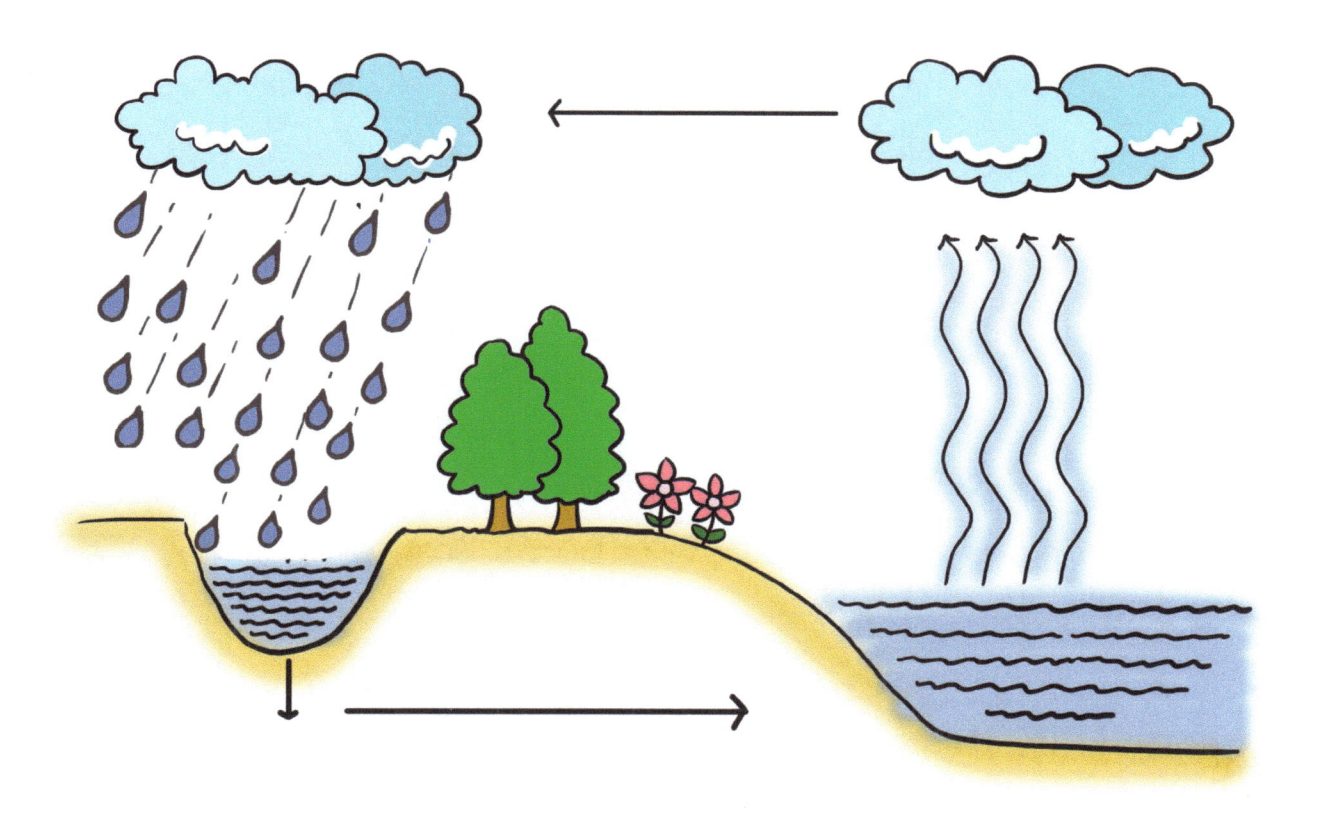

Her aunt said, "This wet air becomes clouds. The clouds move over the land and rain falls from them. That rain fills our lakes. Our drinking water comes from those lakes."

Bess looked at the glass of water she was drinking. "You mean I'm drinking my own tears?" she said, smiling.

Her aunt laughed. "Maybe!"

23

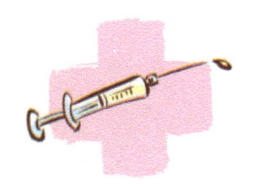

For the Love of Kids

Some people do things for money. But Jonas Salk did things for people. Mr. Salk was born into a poor family. But he studied hard and became a scientist.

At that time, a terrible childhood disease was killing many kids. It was making others very sick and unable to walk.

It was called *polio*. It scared people everywhere. They wanted someone to find a way to protect children from this disease. But that was not easy.

Nevertheless, Jonas Salk worked hard. In 1952, he discovered a vaccination that worked.

Soon, polio began to disappear. The world was very happy. They honoured the great scientist.

Mr. Salk could have made a lot of money from his discovery. But he decided that he did not want to do that. He gave away his discovery for free.

When a writer asked him why, he said, "I want as many kids as possible to get this vaccination. That alone will make me happy."

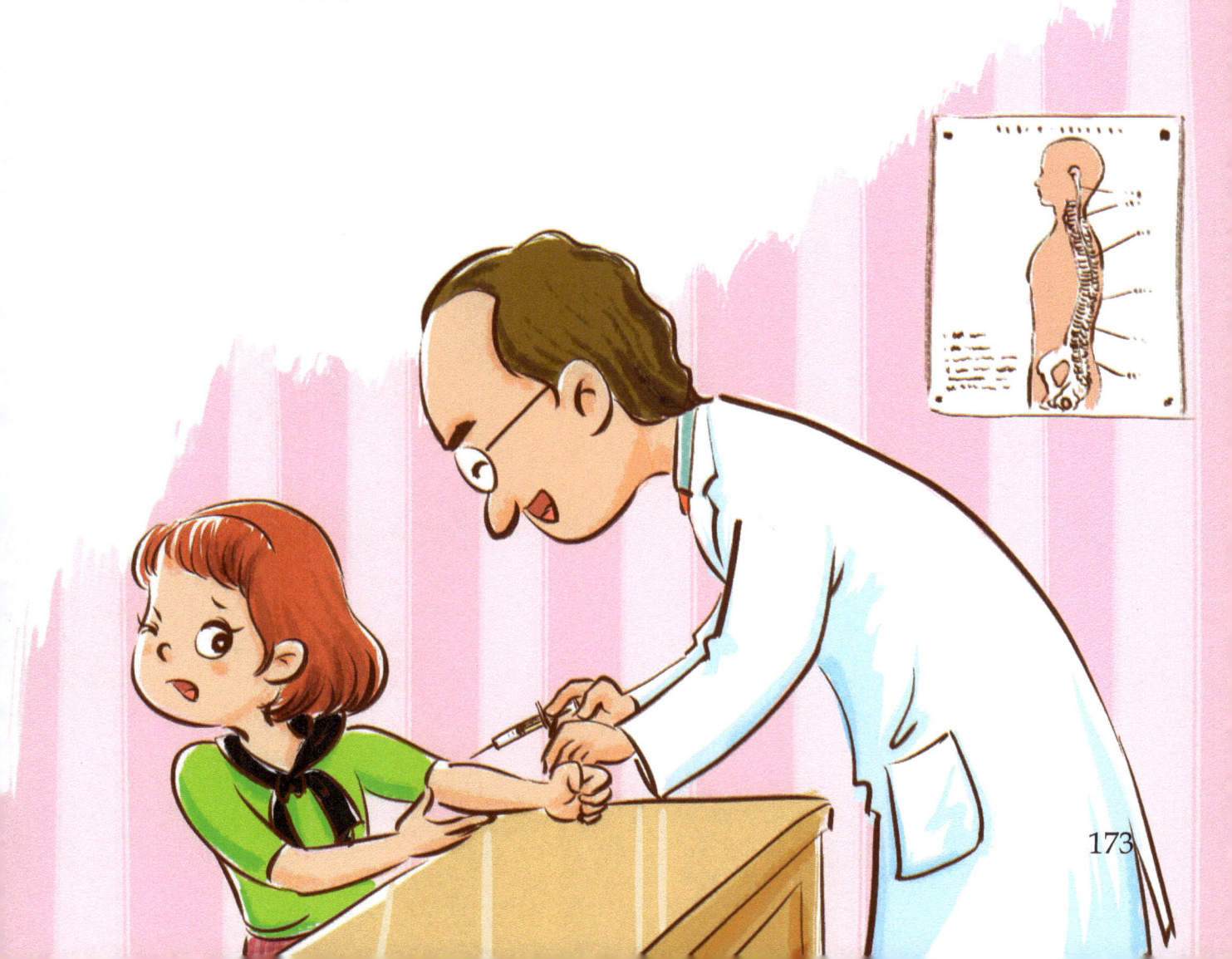

24

What Is Under the Bed?

I'm the youngest girl in my family. My older sisters like scary movies. I do not. But still, I ended up watching a scary movie with them. I was trying to act older.

After the movie, I went right to bed. But I couldn't sleep. Every sound was scary. Finally, I started to fall asleep. But then, I heard a noise under my bed!

I was really scared. I screamed. My whole family came rushing into the bedroom. "What is under the bed?" I yelled.

My dad reached under the bed and pulled out the monster!

I screamed again.

Then I laughed. It was our cat Willy. Dad put Willy on the bed with me. I finally fell asleep.

When I woke up in the morning, I said to my cat, "No more scary movies for me, Willy." I could see that he agreed. It had been a scary night for him too!

25

Two Friends

There were two cats. One was Grey. The other was White.

White lived in a warm house. Every day, he sat by the window, looking outside and feeling all alone. Grey did not have a home. He ran outside catching leaves and chasing mice. He did not have any friends either.

Winter was coming, and the days were getting colder. One day, a door opened. Grey looked in. He saw White looking at him. The house was warm. Grey smelled delicious cat food.

He took a step into the house. Then he took another. Soon he was in the house.

He looked around. It was safe and warm. White walked over. The two touched nose to nose, sniffing each other. Soon, they were cuddled together in the soft cat bed.

26

Happy to Be Busy

Mr. Plano is more than eighty years old. He is healthy and happy. He rarely needs a doctor. What is the trick of keeping old age away from this old man?

He says his trick is "keeping busy".

When you visit his home, you will find a lot of furniture and picture frames. He makes them himself.

Is he a carpenter? No, Mr. Plano is not a carpenter. He was a gym teacher before he retired.

When he retired, he started making furniture. He learned to cut, saw, sand and glue. He loves wood. And he loves woodworking. More importantly, he loves to be busy.

He collects the furniture that people throw away. From these old pieces of furniture, he makes stools, desks, tables and picture frames.

He says he is happy to be as busy as a bee.

27

What Colour Is That?

Allan's father wears a suit with a shirt and tie to work. Sometimes, the shirt is blue. Sometimes, it's green. Sometimes, it's white.

But every morning, he needs Allan's help to get a tie that matches his shirt.

What's the problem?

Allan's father is colour blind. He cannot tell green from red. He cannot tell blue from green.

Nearly one in ten men has some kind of colour-blindness.

The most common kind is red-green. But some people cannot see any colours at all.

Imagine how hard that is!

Think of how dull the world looks to someone who cannot see colours!

Luckily, Allan's father has Allan to help him out. Still, it's a problem he lives with every day.

28

Old Dog, New Tricks

Aunt Lisa is seventy-two years old. She does not own a computer. She sends letters through the post office.

We make fun of her. We tell her that the days of stamps, envelopes and letters are long gone. Still, Aunty says, "It was good enough when I was a girl. It should be good enough now. Besides, you can't teach an old dog new tricks!"

So you can imagine our surprise when we got this email from Aunt Lisa:

Hi Ally and Todd,

As you know, I am travelling in Europe. Are you surprised to get this email? I bet you are. Well, before I left for my vacation, I took some lessons at the Seniors Computer Club. I learned how to send an email. So, I am sending you this message. I changed my mind. You CAN teach an old dog new tricks!

Love,

Aunt Lisa

29

The Little Seeds

One day, Dad asked me to help him plant some green peas. We put them a few inches into the ground. We covered them with soil and watered them.

Every day, I went out to check if anything happened. Days passed and I started to think planting was a waste of time.

Then one day, as I was doing my usual check, I noticed something. There were little green leaves poking out of the soil!

It may seem silly, but it was very exciting to see this!

The seeds we planted turned into plants. And these plants were going to grow sweet little peas. It made me think about how everything grows... even how people grow.

"In some ways, we are not so different from those little peas," I said to my dad. "We need food, water and a place to grow."

I learned a lot from those little seeds.

Snowflakes

Snowflakes come from way up high.
Snowflakes reach us from the sky.

The kids are singing this song. They are singing this song because it's snowing, and they will be going out soon to play in the snow!

Their teacher, Mrs. Austin, knows that her students love the snow.

"Did you know that in one snowstorm, billions of snowflakes fall?" she asks.

"Billions?" The kids are amazed.

"And even more amazing: no two snowflakes look the same. Each snowflake has its own shape. And every snowflake has six sides."

The kids are really excited to learn about snowflakes. Their teacher continues, "Snowflakes are not always white. In places where there is a lot of pollution, snowflakes can be black or grey."

One kid asks, "How fast do snowflakes fall?"

Mrs. Austin smiles. "About 5 kilometres an hour," she says. "Don't worry. You won't get hurt by falling snowflakes. They are gentle and light. Now, let's go out and play!"

Grandma, the Biker

"It's easy!" yelled my older brother. "Anybody can do it!"

Anybody but me. I had a new bike. But, I kept falling off. I was about to give up. Then, my grandmother came outside. "Here, let me show you," she said.

We all said, "No Grandma! You'll fall down. You'll hurt yourself!"

My grandmother is small. But when she wants to do something, you'd better stay out of her way!

My sister helped her get on my bike. Grandma started to pedal. Soon she took off. She rode right down the street. She rode out of sight!

We started to worry. Then, we heard a bell behind us. Grandma had gone all the way around the block!

She got off the bike. "You see," she said. "Once you get it, you'll never forget it!"

My grandma was right. Soon I was riding too… Thanks to Grandma, the biker.

Scan the code to listen to the online audio.

Printed in Poland
by Amazon Fulfillment
Poland Sp. z o.o., Wrocław